Gallery Books
Editor: Peter Fallon

KERRY SLIDES

Paul Muldoon

KERRY SLIDES

with photographs by Bill Doyle

Gallery Books

Kerry Slides
was first published
in a clothbound edition
on 19 April 1996.
First paperback edition
April 1998.

The Gallery Press
Loughcrew
Oldcastle
County Meath
Ireland

ISBN 1 85235 213 2

The Gallery Press acknowledges the financial assistance
of An Chomhairle Ealaíon / The Arts Council, Ireland,
and the Arts Council of Northern Ireland.

for Nuala Ní Dhomhnaill

On a night when a hay-stack, silver-wet,
bulges out from under a fishing-net
so I can barely tell sea from land
I remember the wreckers of Inch Strand

who would gather there on a stormy night
and tie a lantern or hurricane-light
to some wild-eyed pony's mane or tail
that it might flash and flare and flick and flail

like a lantern tied to a storm-tossed mast,
till the captain who'd hoped to escape
Dingle Bay's insidious shallows and shoals

now suddenly found himself foundering, fast,
surrounded by wild-eyed men in capes
wielding pikes and pitchforks and heavy poles.

A Wrenboy's wand clatters down our slates.
It's 1969. A damp
little holiday cottage in Camp.
A few sodden sods of turf in the grate.

I hold the front page
of *The Armagh Observer* to the fireplace.
O dark, dark, dark amid the blaze
of Ian Paisley's face in a blind rage.

In Gleann na nGealt, where the cranks and crazies
were once connoisseurs of watercresses
you still find crackpots, though they're now given
to hitching a horse to a horse-drawn caravan.

At the South Pole Inn
(once owned by Tom Crean)
the ice in your gin
still grumbles and groans.

You still hear the yelps
of phantoms — men, dogs —
crying out for help
through tobacco-fog.

Surely that can't be the high-pitched whistle
that passes for a mating-call
in the Sika deer?
Surely it's March rather than November?

He wraps himself in a hearth rug
charred and singed by load after little load
of red-hot cinders,
by red-hot cinders and white-hot embers.

He holds out a Japanese secateur
to nibble one wallflower high on the wall
of Minard Castle.

He's holding out for all bitter-enders —
the Natterjack toad,
the gadwall, the Greater Spotted slug.

When he shot the gun-running sequence
in *Ryan's Daughter*
David Lean had two fire-engines
trained on his actors.

By which time Nature
must have had enough of being 'enhanced'
at the whim of every film director:
it's been raining ever since.

The plovers come down hard, then clear again,
for they are the embodiment of rain.

Not only do Dingle houses effervesce
like sherbets in rain,
giving one a sense of Fez,

perhaps, or somewhere in Spain,
but I've come upon a ruined shed
at the end of an overgrown lane

with the half-door a rumpled shade
of mint or peach — the jerkin of a fus-
ilier after a fusillade.

This cobalt-quiffed ewe among the fuchsia's
part blue-rinsed Grandmama, part Sid Vicious.

A little west of Dingle is 'The Wood',
one of the very few congregations of trees
that have somehow withstood

the winds that bring most to their knees
along this windswept coast.
A friend who worked for years in forestry

will come here, if he feels downcast,
and himself kneel before the holy rood
of an oak, an ash, a beech, a honey locust.

Ventry Strand. Here Fionn and the Fianna first hurled themselves against the Rest of the World.

Norseman. Norman. Elizabethan knight. All wondered,
as they came down this road in search of plunder,
who could have made such a dreadful blunder:
surely a bridge goes *over* a river, not *under*?

Again and again it comes my turn
to wriggle between the two stone posts
at the mouth of the souterrain

in Dunbeg and I'm beset
by claustrophobia. Yet from the ramparts
of such a fort on such an exposed

headland my ancestors must have peered
across the sea, must have taken into account
a sudden squall of birds

not heard in that part of Connaught —
the '*kee-yah*' of the Arctic tern
or the '*hurrah-hurrah*' of the gannet.

Six sods of turf fell out of Peig's basket.
She bent to gather them up. The Blaskets.

Bhí an seisear againn ag teacht i dtír
i naomhóg Pháidi Mhici Sheáin,
ar rámha fuinnsighe ag tarraingt mar dhaoir
ar bórd loinge Phárthaláin.

I bhfad ó bhaile a bhíonn na hionaidh
ach casadh orainn sa chuas
teach pobail Dhún Chaoin 's slua mór daoine
's greim gliomaigh acu ar chnuas

na farraige — ar na maidí trasna
's na rachtai fír-chleithe 's na caisc fíona
's raic na Spáinne 's bruth Shasana
do bhailigh a sinsir mar abhar díona.

A fisherman nurses his '*Ranga* on the rocks',
the rusty cocktail
named after a shipwreck,
then knocks it back. The actual.

Though it may seem as Irish as Brian Boru
the fuchsia's blown in here from Chile or Peru,
its flower a red flare sent up by the crew

of a sinking ship, the *Montbretia*, whose life-rafts
they lower like buckets into a shaft
where little orange life-vests bob grimly fore and aft.

Why would Tom Ashe
choose, if choose
he did, to be force-fed through a tundish
like a goose?

Why would a British knight
plot to overthrow
those who had violated human rights
in Mayo and the Putumayo?

And why, when he starts the Dingle Regatta
by firing a blunderbuss,
does Charlie Haughey — the erstwhile 'Boss' —
remind me of Buffalo Bill Cody?

SP OFFICE

Seallṫlacaḋóir

ANTIPOST BETTING ON ALL MAJOR EVENTS

HORSES   DOGS   FOOTBALL   POLITICS

Every time I order a bagel with lox and a schmear
in some New York or 'New York style' deli
I leap from the 'lox' in *Leix*lip to the 'schmear' in *Smer*wick
(to the 'butter creek' in the lee of the 'butter mountain')

and the dragon-prowed ships appear
whose end is destruction, I say, whose God is their belly
full of butter and cheese and cream cheese and the extra-thick
milkshakes in a New York or 'New York style' soda fountain.

Earl Grey of Wilton
gnaws at a Stilton
and knocks back some port
as his men poniard
six hundred Spaniards
in the Golden Fort.

Nor can Ed Spenser
be above censure
since he keeps tally,
while the greatest fan
of this scorched earth plan
is Walter Raleigh.

'Out' to the mainland, 'in' to the island,
as the Gaelic
would have it. An old woman in a calico
dress and a blue-suited old man salute

us on the road to Sybil Head. Their hands
have been too long in the bath,
their faces also, while both
her dress and his suit are frowsty with salt.

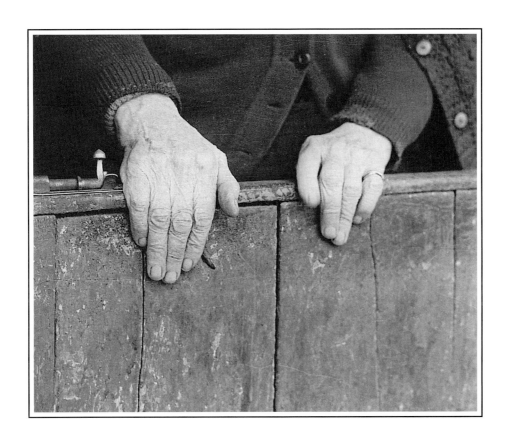

As Jean tried to squeeze through the east window
of the church at Kilmalkedar
I heard a voice. And I followed that voice into
the graveyard to a grave that ran like a gutter

with slurry, to a skeleton, a coarse-seamed skull:
'I am the one of whom Pierce Ferriter
wrote that his heart still smouldered like a coal
on account of her "cold ardour".'

An ogham stone stands four-square as the fridge
I open yet again to forage
for a bottle of Smithwick's or Bass
when 'Beárrthóir means "a barber",' O'Boyle avers,
'but bearradóir in Gortahork
is "a cow that eats at other cows' tails . . ." '
and there's a faint whiff of a chemistry-lab

as through the fridge-door there pass
three old teachers, three philosophers
who followed the narrow track
to the highest good, followed a cattle-trail
to this four-square limestone slab
with one straight edge all notches and nicks:
Sean O'Boyle; John McCarter; Jerry Hicks.

I think then of Jeremiah Curtin
and Cornplanter's son, the great Solomon O'Beal.
They are squatting like twin guardians
of the spirit world. After he had grazed the poll

of a wren with his jagged arrowhead,
Solomon says, it flittered into a corn-plot.
There he found a man, badly hurt,
his scalp gone, the top of his head covered in blood.

The story goes that it was from Brandon Creek
that Brendan 'The Navigator'
set sail in some kind of a hide-covered currach

and, without the benefit of Mercator's
celestial globe, made his way across the ocean
and up the Mississippi to Decatur

(Illinois, that is, not Indiana or Michigan)
to a bar in which Macgillycuddy's Reeks
appeared to him in what he calls 'the vision'.

Twilight. The graveyard at Annascaul.
Its six-foot-high wall
is hardly about
to keep anyone in, and no one out.

From the fort at Caherconree, in which she was immured,
Blathnaid dumped a gallon
of milk in the river, an urgent
signal to Cuchulainn

that the coast was clear and victory
all but assured.
We live downstream from a milk-factory
from which they run off a mangle of milk and detergent.

A Wrenboy's wand clatters down our slates.
Jigs. Reels. Hornpipes. Kerry slides.

DATE DUE

OCT 2 5 2003	